The *Objective* is *Happiness*

The Art and Law of Attraction

by

Thomas Wakefield

A PRACTICAL GUIDE TO PERSONAL SUCCESS

Wakefield Solutions

Tradepaper ISBN: 978-0-9822397-5-9
Hardcover ISBN: 978-0-9822397-4-2
Spiralbound ISBN: 978-0-9822397-2-8
eBook ISBN: 978-0-9822397-3-5

Library of Congress Control Number: 2008932824

PRINTED IN THE UNITED STATES OF AMERICA

The Objective is Happiness
is dedicated to
Оля
who is my happiness!

*"A powerful force is at work
in your life now.
This force is infinite power,
and unlimited resource."*
— Thomas Wakefield

Table of Contents

Introduction xiii
Prologue xix

Chapter One 1
How Life Is Energy

Chapter Two 3
Thoughts & Feelings

Chapter Three 11
Internal, External & Middle Neighborhoods

Chapter Four 27
Words & Rhythm

Chapter Five 37
See, Hear, Feel, Describe

Chapter Six 45
Cornerstone of the Mechanics, Intention

Chapter Seven... 57
The Soup

Chapter Eight 63
State of Mind & Awe

Chapter Nine 67
Exercises

Chapter Ten 79
Strategies, Be Do Have

Chapter Eleven 83
Perspectives & Accountability

Chapter Twelve 87
I Am & Affirmations

Chapter Thirteen 91
Review

Chapter Fourteen 95
Change

Epilogue 99

Recommended Health 103

Recommended Reading 105

Recommended Watching 107

My Book of Gratitude 111
reference Chapter Three

My Book of Attention 115
reference Chapter Three

My Book of Awe 119
reference Chapter Eight

Table of Contents

My Book of Evidence 123

Chapter Start Quote Credits 127

Acknowledgments 131

About the Author 133

Introduction

The Objective is Happiness is about being, doing, and having the things in your life which are happiness for you.

In living the life you wish to live, understanding subjective energy and being a master of describing what is truly in your heart will get you farther in your desired results faster.

As a point of reference, we will create a Saturday morning state of mind. From this we create and sustain the things which are happiness for us; a state of mind in which your week is done, no demands are being made on you. It is a state of mind where you do what you want and feel how you wish to feel. It is a state of mind where you mind the state of your affairs.

What is becoming known as the "law of attraction" is the most natural aspect of life. Just like gravity or weather, it is an "is." Perhaps you have come across (and perhaps studied) this "law." I am of the opinion people peddling "the law" have been stuck long enough. Let us coin here, or re-coin if you will, to the "art of attraction," demystify and get on with this fascinating life creation stuff.

In talking about "the law of attraction" we use terminology such as, the law or universe listens to you and I, and matches our energy good or bad, and that it listens to and matches us. This manner of describing that law and how it works is convenient and useful for teaching and talking about it.

The fact of the matter is, this multidimensional universe of intelligence we all live in is infinite potential, all possibilities, all frequencies, hence all vibration and whatever we hold in our mind and heart does cause vibration and the corresponding stuff into existence.

This vibrational intelligence matches your thoughts, feelings, intentions, listens to your command, and will control your actions.

The basics are a good place to start. Chapter one says it all. Chapter two is a simple explanation. Chapters three and the others build on and explore fundamentals of how life and language work together.

You can apply what you discover inside and on these pages to more success and new successes in any aspect of your life, and have more of nearly anything you desire.

Introduction

Some readers will use this book as a cookbook, meaning a book of recipes and formulas, others will consider it philosophy and a way to live life, and some readers both.

I mean this to be the shortest comprehensive self-help or motivational book of guidance ever written, and as such, the most concise and powerful. Herein are the understandable basics. The basics being self evident and/or transparent require little explanation, and leave plenty of room for discovery and development. You will easily move beyond basics to artful creation.

We all have friends and neighbors around us who seem to lived charmed lives. Do they know how they do it? My answer is some maybe, but mostly, "no," they do not. On another hand, how many people believe in Jesus, God, Buddha, Lao Tse, rainbows or butterflies, and their lives are a mess? Many of these people are most sincere, authentic, and suffer lack in even the basics of food, housing and transportation. I must presume they know not either. We all develop habits. Read these pages and you will know.

All my life I have been interested in matters of the mind, spirituality, human betterment, how the mind applies to results, and what makes things happen. This interest has brought me into contact with some very interesting people.

I was privileged to know a woman named Virginia Satir

years back, and I like to think she's looking over my shoulder and smiling in approval of this work. Virginia was a highly effective communicator and with her skills, a successful family therapist.

A rather sharp man in her office noticed particular consistencies in how Virginia was getting her rather impressive results. The man, Richard Bandler, was paying attention while Virginia was just plain good at doing what she did in her family therapy practice! Virginia just did what she did in a fashion sometimes labeled unconscious competent (from the conscious competence learning model). Richard figured out how the success she was having was happening. This, by the way, is where NLP, Neuro Linguistic Programming, was born, Virginia's office. The world owes Richard Bandler a debt of gratitude, along with the man he teamed up with, John Grinder, which is another story.

Virginia and I sat around on my patio in the '80's talking of bridge builders and barrier builders, and other communications stuff. Those basics are all here. You have all you need in this book. In the larger picture this book is mostly a reminder and perspective for you. When communication works life works.

What motivated me to write this book was reading and listening to books containing "the secret." I would pick up a book, read, and sometimes wonder how it ever got to print. On another hand, I would watch Wayne Dyer hit it out of the park over and over. I listened to Rhonda's secret, and I am here to tell you "how life works" is not a secret, has never been a secret, and no one was ever trying to keep it from you, not even the leaders of the past (thank you Dennis). All anyone ever really had to do was, and is, pay attention and be of a positive attitude. The only problem is no one ever told us how to pay attention.

If someone says, "What is there to be excited about?" The answer is, "You pick!" The trick, in any aspect of life, is where to place your attention, on what, when, how and, of course, how much attention to pay to what. The answer to that is, pay attention as best you can, keep paying attention and you will improve.

Another motivating point for writing this book was, too many of this type of offering, some loaded with gems, stated the gem and kept going on and on when they should have left you to your own joy of discovery rather than muddy the waters. Also, I have wanted to write something like this again after a long time. Apologies If I'm late.

Which reminds me to mention an author who's writings have meant a lot to me, Richard Bach. There are others, like Carlos Castaneda and Anthony Robbins, yea firewalks!

I have many people to thank. My favorite Kahuna, Joel Pahukula, for Huna training. Chris Christenson with whom I've spent more hours in airplanes than anyone else, mostly float planes; he must get credit for his inspiration, perspective, influence, and as a very best friend.

I have been blessed with many friends and acquaintances, and I am not done yet. Perhaps you and I will meet and become acquainted!

Seeing as how we can always talk more later, my great challenge will be to write just enough... I'll stop this here. You read the prologue and take over!

Prologue

I expect these pages to be refreshing for you, and fun! After all the objective is to create happiness!

A powerful force is at work in your life right now! This force is infinite and it is an unlimited resource. Nothing in your life is more involved with you. This force is freely available. It is already working, you can control it with your awareness of it and how it works.

Read this book like a detective. Any small part may be exactly what you need to make that perfect positive shift in your life.

The Objective is Happiness is written to give you more understanding and structure on how to live, and what you want to live, than anything previously assembled between two covers. The really great news is that so much of this is simple basics.

Some is written in the first person for you, the reader, to read as if the words are your own.

Mark the pages special to you. Date your margin notes. Your order of awareness is your own. You may enjoy looking back over your history of awareness and development.

Chapter one, as you will see, is brief and if you take your time with it, the chapter says it all. Chapter two sets up perspective and begins the process of understanding and focus. The rest of the book is just more strategic perspective, fine-tuning and perhaps inspiration.

I suggest turning the pages slowly from front to back the first time, and after that jump around and re-sequence whatever you want. You will know your strong points and where you want to improve. Perhaps you would team up with a friend; the buddy system works!

So, the objective is happiness. Happiness is that which makes one feel good and causes no harm. The objective result is directly related to the clarity with which an individual can state or describe that which is desired, which in turn affects the timing, speed, and quality of delivery. Clear thought and strength of feelings will enhance this process and your results.

You and I, given just some kind of common circumstances growing up, have been living our lives all our lives. We have been accepting and rejecting ideas, conditions, and situations since we had the ability to make a choice. The first choices were probably between either something feels good or something feels bad. Later on, with perhaps our development of abstract thinking, the evolution was to, "I'd like to try this, or that," contrasted with, "I am going to stay away from that or those!" Or, "I'd rather hang out with certain people than other people."

When in our lives have we not been comparing things we became aware of and probably classifying them? Have you noticed you go through life comparing and classifying, such as, "What's on sale? What food do I like? He/she sure is good looking. Wow, Dad sure is happy today. Look at those kittens tear around! I like this better than that. I'll have one of those!"

We make decisions about what is acceptable and what is not. This is not a secret. Sometimes we have feelings about things. No secret there!

This book is about managing all those notions, options, and opinions to your benefit.

"In the beginning was the Word, and the Word was with God, and the Word was God." John 1:1 (KJV)

"In the beginning God created the heaven and the earth." Genesis 1:1 (KJV)

"And God said, 'Let us make man in our image, after our likeness; and let them have dominion over the fish of the sea, and over the fowl of the air, and over the cattle, and over all the earth, and over every creeping thing that creepeth upon the earth.'" Genesis 1:26 (KJV)

"So God created man in His own image, in the image of God He created him; male and female He created them." Genesis 1:27 (KJV)

"And God blessed them, and God said unto them, 'Be fruitful, and multiply, and replenish the earth, and subdue it; and have dominion over the fish of the sea, and over the fowl of the air, and over every living thing that moveth upon the earth.'" Genesis 1:28 (KJV)

You are created in the likeness of divinity. God's love for you is built into the blessing. So, now you've been blessed and the Word is with you.

This is your life, and it is probably not just yours. I mean you have people who love and care about you. That matters. They matter! You matter to them! Then again, this is your life.

Live life by random chance or live life deliberately.

Grab a pencil and write on these pages as you read. Make notes in the margins! Shape your life intentionally. Near the back of this book you will find lined pages to easily start your own journals on a couple of the important subjects within. The journals are for focussing and reflecting.

Prologue

The Force is with you! You and this Force are one.

Chapter 1
How Life is Energy

"My father says almost the whole world is asleep. Everybody you know, everybody you see, everybody you talk to. He says that only a few people are awake and they live in a state of constant total amazement."[1]

– Meg Ryan

I have what my energy is on.

I do what my energy is on.

I am what my energy is on.

Chapter 2
Thoughts & Feelings

"All that we are is a result of what we have thought."[2]

— Buddha

Welcome to Saturday morning!
(a concept and a state of mind)

My energy is my feelings and my thoughts.

Thoughts are focus. My thinking is my focus.

Emotion is power. My feelings are my power.

Putting this Together

Focus is the most valuable commodity in life. Focus can be taught and developed. Nothing in this life is more useful or valuable than focus.

Feelings are the most powerful commodity in life. Feelings can be understood, developed, and controlled. Nothing in this life is more effective than feelings directed. Consider focussed passion in action!

We need focus, then we can do something on purpose with our energy. Focus can be choosing a direction, a goal, a plan, a style, an attitude. To choose something to the exclusion of other choices is focus. Focus is choice. Focusing is choosing. If I choose to go east, I have eliminated south, west and north.

What in this life is more important than emotional awareness and control? Unfocussed energy can be dangerous. (As can be focused energy) If a person is all charged up on some nasty undesirable, the negative energy can easily get bigger, may explode, and maybe worse, carry over to something or someone else.

We should not be as interested in what people think as much as we are in how they feel, and particularly how they feel about a good thing. Having feelings about good things makes life easy.

Being aware of the strength of your feelings about the objects of your attention is important, because that is where you and universal energy are creating.

An interesting example of focus going wrong is someone of good intention, having a very strong feeling about a bad thing. This is worse than a person who casually likes the bad thing. The good intentions person is having bigger energy on the bad thing. The bad thing is unintentionally fed.

The object of your attention is where your energy goes. Whether you are screaming, "no, no, no," or "yes, yes, yes," matters not. Nope! Either way the screaming is a whole bunch of energy feeding the object of your focus.

Hence, screaming, "I don't want to be fat," or "I don't want to be broke," gets you a whole lot more of being fat or broke!

If you do not want to be picked on, take your thoughts, words and energy off, "stop picking on me!!!" You do not want your energy on the abuse! What you want is respect! Put your feelings and thoughts on, "I am respected."

Practice self respect. In conversation state that you deserve and wish respect, and you would prefer to be treated with respect.

Spend much less time and energy on what you do not want and a whole lot of time and energy on what you do want!!!

Fear and excitement are interesting in this way. Imagine this, imagine yourself standing atop a thirty-foot cliff about to dive into the water below. People have been jumping right here for longer than anyone knows. Ten-year-old kids jump. Sixty-year-old adults jump. You see them jumping and having a good time. You hear laughter and happiness. Now, it's your turn! Is that fear or excitement you're feeling about your jump?

The same physiological stuff, body sensations, adrenalin flow, and what-have-you, go on in your body ether way. The energy is the energy. The difference is in how you label it. And you get to label these things however you want. So, is the example situation panic or excitement? Which do you prefer? What is the story you tell yourself?

Now you can easily understand why we are not at all interested in supporting how you feel about what you say you do not want. Very bad idea to have strong feelings on what you do not want! Why ever would you want to feed the enemy? Feed your friend! Your friend is happiness!

If a problem exists, feed the solution.

What we are most interested in is how good you and everyone can and do feel about what makes us happy! The objective!

Other words related to **focus** are, **desire**, **vision**, **will**, **purpose**, **intention** and many more.

You control and direct energy with your focus and discipline, again, also known as intent, intention, will, prayer, considering, contemplation and those other words.

Thoughts & Feelings

You can also wonder... wonder how good, how soon, how big, how wonderful. Let wonder open your mind and heart, and rev up your energy! Wonder is a powerful tool for your advantage!

So, what's on your mind, and how strong are your feelings about it? What do you want to feed with your life energy?

Take a minute, write some things right here.

What are a few of the simplest things that give you happiness? What brings a tear to your eye? What gets you to give your loudest cheer? For what are you most grateful? Write a few things you can be happy about.

_____

_____

_____

_____

_____

_____

I wonder how wonderful and exciting _____

_____ is?!!!

The Objective is Happiness

I wonder _____?!

_____ is what I wonder about most.

How is your confidence? What is your level of confidence? What will you allow? If you want, you can be more and more clever about this. What is your style of energy? Are you free to have fun? The objective is happiness! People like me! People respect me!

Fill in the spaces with what feels good. What makes you smile? What makes you happy? What if you were young or old and free to write anything?

Take a moment right here, or take a few days. Write your things which are or would be happiness for you.

1. _____

2. _____

3. _____

4. _____

5. _____

6. _____

7. _____

8. _____

9. _____

Meditation, by the way, is nothing other than when your mind is not being like a monkey cage. One reason to meditate is to develop focus. Meditation (for the most part) is quieting the mind, letting go of the "noise", steering the mind, pointing it to something, a focus.

Reasons to meditate are to simply relax your mind and body, calm down, take a breath. Tame the monkeys!

Quality of Energy

Let's address quality of energy. Energy has infinite ways to exist and express. Fire, as an example of energy, can be a raging expression or it can be a slow long low steady type of energy.

Dramatic is a type of energy and has certain characteristics. It can be loud and animated. Subtle is a type of energy and has other qualities. Subtle by its nature is not obvious, but can be hugely powerful.

Confidence as an energy has a certain quality inherent in its state. Belief is powerful energy. Knowing is the best energy.

Intuitively we are aware of many types and styles of energy. The variety in types and styles of energy is infinite. All we have to do to know energy types is pay attention.

Types and qualities of energy is worth the study. Study and discover options for yourself.

Chapter 3
Internal, External & Middle Neighborhoods

"Our attitude toward life determines life's attitude toward us."[3]

– Earl Nightingale

Remember, the premise is we can, and do constantly, create and recreate our reality. Let's address the internal and external you. External is outside you and internal is inside.

We could say, we have our inner neighborhood and our outer neighborhood.

In regard to our outer neighborhood, we never quite know who'll come knocking on our door. That is the nature of living life as part of society. The phone rings.

The mail arrives. You're at the grocery store. You have neighbors as part of your outer neighborhood. Some live next door and others on the other side of the planet.

Then we also have our inner neighborhood. We have much broader control and more ease in control over our inner neighborhood. You think about what you want to think about and feel on your schedule. You can think of your inner neighborhood as your personal living Garden of Eden.

Our five senses have an inner and outer aspect.

Your emotions and feelings are internal, unless and until you express them outwardly. Also you can "feel" the warm sun on your face, an external sensation of feeling. So, feelings are both inside and outside. Your emotions are inside and if you want, you can express them outwardly. You choose who may know how much and what you are feeling.

Of course you can see with your physical eyes, and in your mind's eye is your inner vision. You can hear with the ears on the side of your head; you also have an inner ear and you have an inner voice.

If you wonder about this inner voice, just be quiet and listen. If you happen to think, "Voice? What voice? I don't hear any voice, seems pretty quiet in here," that's the voice! Those words are from inside you, your inner voice heard by your inner ear.

The Importance of Inside

Inside us is where things come from. Our beliefs and attitudes are what attract all things to us. Your inner world is the place of cause.

Happiness is an inside job. Feelings of emotion are one thing and physical feelings are something else. Feeling good is one thing and a good feeling is another, and a physical feeling is yet another.

A stiff muscle is a feeling from within your body. It is a physical feeling and not to be confused with an internal feeling of some emotion.

There are no external feelings of emotion, there are external expressions of emotion. Emotions internally expressed show up in illness or wellness.

So, while a touch can feel good, the "feeling of good," is internal.

The Importance of Gratitude

Here may be the most important paragraph in this book. You have a powerhouse feeling within which will lend to creating all good things! It is gratitude. Feel gratitude! The simple state of feeling grateful. Study gratitude, practice, and develop your feelings of gratitude. Be and feel grateful for every possible thing you can dream up. *"It's all good!"* — C.K.

For an example, I am grateful for grass. What is better than the smell of a new-mowed lawn on a pleasant summer morning? There are many. I go out in the country to ride my bike slowly by new-mowed hay fields for that magnificent smell of new-mowed hay. Then there's also that week of plum blossoms every spring. You can go as basic as being grateful for dirt.

If you can be in a constant state of gratitude, then your energy with the energy of God multiplied, creates and feeds only good things.

As I write this on a warm spring day sitting in my 4th floor Nikolaev, Ukraine apartment, no kidding, I hear someone playing a piano in the distance. The music is pleasant and I am grateful. Always, I pay attention! The world around delights me.

The book you should write on gratitude (and you should write it), could be your most important writing. Write everything which touches you in a positive fashion. Perhaps you would categorize, because you will likely find this exercise never ending! A starter journal is near the back of this book.

We create our reality inside and outside from within ourselves. We do this from our attitudes, desires, and all those things we think and say and have feelings about. Our feelings are part and parcel with our convictions. Convictions, confidence and belief all weave the tapestry of our life.

What is the story you tell yourself about how life works? Do you tell yourself life is hard, grueling, got to work overtime, dues paying then all you get is a gold watch situation? Or, do you tell yourself life is an adventure, lots of fun, and no matter what comes up I always win situation?

Remember, every thought with a little or a lot of feeling creates or nurtures something. You are creating and recreating, or sustaining something even as you read this.

Congruency and Contrast

Here I can introduce congruency. Happiness in your heart and a smile on your face is an example of inner and outer congruence. Congruency is things in harmony or matching.

Congruency is powerful! Congruency will get you more of what you have. Congruency with bad things is more of bad, and congruency with good things is more of good. Again, congruency is excellent for enhancing what you have. Like attracts like.

Congruency as a good thing is good for enhancing that which you wish improved.

Congruency can be contrasted with contrast. One example of contrast is having the little angel on one shoulder and the little devil on the other.

One might be saying, "All is well. Go for it!" The other says, "Do you think that is wise?" Who said which? Which one's talking anyway?

For assistance, ask someone who believes in you! Ask someone who validates themselves and validates you. You do not have friends who invalidate you! A person who invalidates you is not your friend.

When we have clear contrast we see things better. In our auditory world we have harmony and discord; we hear when things sound funny or sound true. In our kinesthetic feeling world we have that gut feeling of knowing right and wrong.

If life is terrible and one is depressed, may I suggest contrast?

Contrast is excellent for making choices. You will find a great change exercise in the chapter on exercises. The exercise uses contrast.

Your feelings can be affected by external stimulus, or not! You have a choice! If some idiot says you're stupid, what is the value of the comment? Then again, if get I a compliment from a person I respect, I'll allow it. I may even take it to heart! Mom always said, *"Consider the source."* — Willie Wakefield

Pay attention to life; make choices! If there is a diary to keep, it is the *How I Pay Attention to Life* diary, authored by you. This is Volume Two of your My Life Library, on the shelf right next to your *My Book of Gratitude*.

To make things easier on ourselves we can make a couple of fundamental decisions and build a foundation for life on two basic attitudes.

First Fundamental Attitude Question

"Is this universe, I live and move and breathe in, a friendly place or an adversarial place?"

Remember, with this answer you make a fundamental choice and are creating a foundation in your life (from the question by Albert Einstein).

You are, right now, creating, recreating or sustaining with this decision!

What you will fundamentally attract, at the most basic level, will be congruent with your decision here. The decision is effective immediately. The results will show up in time congruent with your conviction. Which do you prefer, friendly or adversarial?

Inner World - Outer World

This choice will dictate your most basic attitude. Your choice sets the stage. This attitude is the general makeup of your inner neighborhood.

This creation of your inner world should be deliberate. You may have read, *"As above, so below," and, "as within, so without."* Credit for this goes to Hermes.

Create your inner world with your intention that your outer world match! Hold the vision and intention and your outer world will match your inner world more and more closely. Be clear and be deliberate.

Considering cause and effect, your inner world is cause, and you find the effects in your outer world.

Is your inner space a happy place? What are the attitudes and truths inside you? What is important and what is of value?

I am not saying live only in a dream world. Be alive inside and out! Pay attention to your inner and outer worlds, and always to what you prefer in each. Be active in each!

Let me interrupt for one paragraph to say, the thing commonly referred to as the "law of attraction" should be referred to as the "art of attraction." There is a law and the application of it is so extensive we can easily use the word art. This law or art does not require drums and horns and gongs or "secret givers." This law or art of attraction is not your God-given "right", this is simply your God-given "how life works." Cause and effect in life is simple. Your inner world is cause, and within your outer world are the effects.

This law of creation is just life, and how life works. The art work is up to you!

What you give your feelings and focus to, is what happens in your life!

We decide to what we are attracted and what we are attracted to we give energy. This energy creates, recreates, or sustains. And in turn, we attract more of the same.

Like attracts like. When we set up a cycle, or a habit, the energy keeps going around and around. Think about repetition in your life, and why things probably stay the same.

"Yes" and "no" energy is not a problem if you know how to work each to your advantage, particularly the "no" energy. You need not work so hard managing this use of words and energy.

Learn to say, "yes." We have a way to eliminate "no." If something is a "no," then something else is more desirable and therefore a "rather." What are your "rathers?"

Do I want to be picked on? "No!" I would much rather be respected! So, eliminate "no" and give your energy to those things you would "rather" experience. You can always say, "no, I would rather..." Rather is a strategy fundamental to our art of attraction getting us to "yes."

"No" is really a great word and concept and energy when it is used with rather. What you are doing here is redirecting rather than trying to stop something. Redirecting energy is much easier and more fun. Ask a kung fu instructor.

Mainly, we want to stay away from "no!" giving any energy to that which you do not want. With this "rather" strategy, you have a way of always landing on your "Yes."

Second Fundamental Attitude Question

This brings us to the second fundamental question and decision. The, "who am I? Am I good enough? Do I deserve the best life has to offer? Am I competent? Am I Ok?"

Your answer better be a huge, "Yes!"

Why? Go to the basic! You are attracting and creating now with every thought and feeling! "I am" statements are very very powerful statements of now.

The answer is from the basic "where you focus your energy is what is created." You are, and will be having, doing, and being what your energy is on.

What your energy is on now is/are the coming attractions in your life! Always (the) now!!!

We have a great deal of power and focus in "I am" statements. I am statements assume "now" and they state what "is."

What list of good "I am" traits can you write for yourself? Start making that list and make it and remake it. Making this list right now is a good idea! On this page write at least one nice "I am" about you right here in the spaces.

I am _____

I am _____

I am _____

I am _____

Write a bunch of these all over this page.

Yes, you can get there from here. You can get anywhere from anywhere. Wherever a person is in their experience or development is not as important as comprehending where or how they want to be!

Earl Nightingale says, *"Picture yourself in your mind's eye as having already achieved this goal. See yourself doing the things you'll be doing when you've reached your goal."*

All you need do is comprehend, even a little bit, being where you want to be and the experience of that! Comprehend as if the thing is arriving or already exists. Conduct yourself as if the thing is a part of your life now. What does it feel like? What does it look and sound like? Does it have any smell or taste?

Worth a note, *"Jesus said to them, 'Because of your unbelief; for truly I say to you, If there is faith in you even as a grain of mustard seed, you will say to the mountain, move away from there, and it will move away; and nothing would prevail over you.'"*

— Matthew 17:20 (Lamsa)

Do you have the faith of a mustard seed? A mustard seed is very small. So the point is if you can maintain even a small amount of faith, you can realize what your energy is on. Faith is defined as complete trust or confidence or strong belief. Belief is defined as an acceptance that a statement is true.

If you think you should count beads, sit in certain postures, meditate and such for enlightenment, or living what you wish, that is okay too!

Remember what the *Messiah's Handbook* says, *"Argue for your limitations, and sure enough, they're yours."*
Illusions, The Adventures of a Reluctant Messiah
— Richard Bach

Now is the moment of creation! Flip the switch!

And let me add that counting, sitting, breathing and tai chi, martial arts and training and challenging ourselves in whatever fashions are really great things. These things give life richness, texture and meaning to both our outer and inner life. Achievement certainly supports happiness.

Maybe sometimes some feel the need to pay dues, maybe. One certainly does not have to pay dues for good moods, attitudes, joy, happiness, or gratitude. The practice of good moods will get you a long way toward real world happiness. If you have a notion you must pay dues for something, please set the price you are willing to pay!

Life being an inside to outside creation, meaning we are creating our circumstances and conditions from within ourselves, means we should pay attention to our perceptions at all times. If you are going to pay one way or another, pay attention.

Notice that you notice things. Your mental wandering spreads energy. Your gaze is giving energy to that which it falls upon. The things you have feelings about are receiving energy.

You are a sower of seeds constantly energizing that which comes into your field of attention.

Your focus, feelings, and decisions give, direct, and redirect energy. Decisions give life to answers and results happen.

So, a really important question is, "Am I happy?" "Deep down inside... am I happy?" This is important because your deep down inside energy affects everything.

Middle Neighborhood

For simplicity, let us address our human body as a bridge from our inner world to our outer world and refer to it as our middle world.

We have a most intimate relationship with our body. Or should I write our body has a most intimate relationship with us? The answer is both. While those around us may not be privy to our thoughts and feelings, none of our thoughts or feelings escape recognition by our body!

The correlations should be obvious. For example, the depressed person probably does not stand straight or have a spring in their step.

People who take pride in themselves will live a happy and spirited life, will be healthier, happier, and have more likelihood of a longer life and a younger look.

By their fruits ye shall know them. Also by their glow, their tone of voice, the subject matter of their conversation. "By their fruits" has many applications. If you walk your talk, you are probably good for your word. All these various "fruits" are indications of an organized inner world. What matters to you? What do you believe? What do you stand by?

Doctors and nurses tell themselves stories of health, as do sick people. Different stories! Medical people can be around the sick day in and day out and are very rarely ill.

Please read and understand the following paragraph. It is important to understanding the object of what our energy is on.

Are your thoughts and feelings on whether or not you want to be fat? Or? Are your thoughts and feelings on whether or not you want to be fit?

Do you understand the distinction? This difference should be, or become, as obvious to you as dark differs from high noon.

Consider that your body picks up on its environment, inner and outer. It is constantly reading the totality of your beingness, mentally, emotionally, spiritually, physical and environmental.

Something in you regulates heart rate, breathing, balance, hydration, blood and cleansing, digestion, cell division, healing and how many other systems?

On another level, I listen to music. It goes in my ears, then what happens? Why do I like good old time rock and roll, and opera? Why does the sight of my sweetheart smiling bring me such joy?

The point is you and I have many levels of beingness

and each is a miracle. When we meet I will look upon you with awe! And I will wonder what matters to you.

I am astounded by this thing we call life! I live in constant awe. The subject could be dirt, the subject could be love. Wow. :-)

Consider further that your body picks up on your thoughts and feelings, and is affected by your attitude. When one thinks evil and permeates themselves with negative music they are in effect contributing to their own suicide. Science and medicine will figure out what bad thought equals what bad condition someday.

Respecting and taking good care of your body is imperative in your application of your energy. If you wish to be respected and healthy, in all manner, you must respect yourself. Practice self-respect toward impeccability. Your basic attitudes and such do affect your health, well-being and success.

As long as you're at it, respect others. Having read this far, you know things they probably do not know, not consciously anyway. Cut them some slack. It's part of that what goes around comes around thing.

Find ways to be grateful.

Chapter 4
Words & Rhythm

"Within you now and always is the unborn possibility of a limitless experience of inner stability and outer treasure, and yours is the privilege of giving birth to it."[4]

— Eric Butterworth

Consider your life as a song – a song with music and lyrics. Your song has a rhythm and it has a chorus. We must pay attention to our inner music and words, especially our chorus which repeats over and over.

Your music is your mood, general attitude, goals, and all. It is your life. It should be something like, "people like me, good things happen to me, my life is charmed, I am competent. I am confident! Good fortune surrounds me! I am happy! I am okay!"

Your other words are your lyrics which are your focus,

goals, or desires, affirmations and such. Lyrics could be your kind of success, adventures, conditions, and/or whatever situations you like to live.

You choose the words because you are the one who assigns meaning and gives meaning, to all things in your life.

And there's always the popular lyric, "I always get the front parking space!"

The last line in the movie, *Being There*, Chance, the Peter Sellers character hears, *"After all... life is a state of mind."* You should choose your own state of mind because, if you do not choose your own, circumstances or peers will hand you one.

Many of us pick up our attitudes which are states of mind, from parents and peers. How often is that a good idea? I choose my beliefs and attitudes.

I want to choose my life. I will say what is acceptable and unacceptable! I choose my adventures.

Let's explore these "musical" choices.

So, let's say your life is a song. You choose the music and you write the lyrics.

Write some "I am" statements about yourself. You can pretend if you want. These words are words of "making", you are creating yourself. You can also be recreating, refining or fine tuning yourself. Start from scratch, keep only what you wish, modify where you will, do what you want.

I am loved, I am creative, I am reliable, I am very good in a romantic relationship, I am enthusiastic, I am a good person, I am happy.

Your words, the words you use, are bringing things into your life and keeping things out of your life.

Let's start with the subject you! So these sentence thoughts may all start with "I".

Our main focus is the object of the sentence/thought.

The object of your thought must be your desired state or result. That is where energy is flowing.

You do not want any energy on things you have decided against or made no particular choice on.

Here is what happens with a bad energy strategy. "I don't (or do not) want to be fat!" Let's exaggerate to make a good point. **"I absolutely am sick and tired of clothes not fitting, people snickering behind my back, and feeling second or third rate, I do not want to be fat!!!!!"**

Okay, I get that you would like to be thin. There are also

three other objects of your energy in that sentence. But, you have a single problem. The problem is how the energy works, which is simple.

What the object of that thought really and energetically is, **"I [whole bunch of energy] fat!"**

Also note clothes not fitting, people snickering, and feeling third rate got all the energy also. Correct focus is so easy and necessary.

What you want in this example is thin, fit, energetic, happy and such. So the focus is, **"I [whole bunch of energy] physically fit !!!"**

Here's an example. **"I am absolutely certain and sure I feel better with more energy being fit and thin!!!"**

Your energy gives life to, and feeds, the object of your focus. Be careful what you feed, it might just come true.

With your attention, emotion, and words you are creating at all times whether they are spoken or thought. The spoken word can be more powerful than a thought and the written word more powerful yet. So, obviously a good strategy is to think desirable things, write them and say them, and write them and say them again.

If you simply have a casual comment type of thought in the privacy of your own mind you are "feeding" something. If you have feelings or attitude about this thought, how strong is the energy? How well are you feeding it? Remember, repetitious small thoughts give lots over time.

The things people gossip and gripe about are very well fed. By the way, some people sense this subjective energy and feed on it themselves. Many are unconscious about what is going on and some know exactly what is happening.

This is true in both desirable and undesirable subjects. Some people are unconscious of this energy thing when nurturing you or upsetting you, and some others know quite exactly what is going on when they nurture you or push your buttons.

My best suggestion for friendship is spend your time and energy with people who validate you at your best. Reject those who invalidate your goodness. I live by this! An important point is you must validate yourself!

Back to the music!

Write several "I am" statements regarding your self and character which will be the music.

- I am honorable.
- I am respected.
- I am generous.
- I am a great friend.
- I am romantic.
- I am fun.

- I am compassionate.
- I am creative.
- I am loved.
- I am okay.
- I am caring.
- I am considerate.

What are some of yours?

- I am _____

- I am _____

- I am _____

- I am _____

Those I am statements are the foundation you live from, can always fall back on, and build on, to maintain the life which is your happiness.

Time for a good question. **"What do I allow?"** Related questions are: where do I nurture and support, and where do I sabotage those things that would bring me joy? Where am I building bridges in my life? Where do I build barriers?

Now let's write the "I" statements of conditions and situations which are the words of my song. These are statements which are true or I would be happy to have be true.

- I [energy] physicaly fit!
- I [energy] happy!
- I [energy] good job!
- I [energy] special relationship(s).
- I [energy] security.

- I _____

- I _____

- I _____

- I _____

- I _____

"I am so happy and grateful that my friends hold me in such high regard!"

"I always find the best deal!"

"I am in awe of my life!"

"I experience _____ "

"I attract _____ "

"I enjoy _____ "

"I am" statements are only one type of affirmation. The object in your thought need not necessarily be at the end of a sentence. Your thoughts need not be all "I am" statements. You just need to know what the object is.

In paying attention to creating your life with these words of making the time is always now. The life you live is now, nothing else! **Seize the moment!**

Of course in your day-to-day life you schedule a dental appointment, mark your calendar for your next lunch date, and make out a guest list and a shopping list for the holiday dinner. These are things you do in passing in your life.

The lyrics of your song are the larger life you live, and do affect the errands you run and passing activities. Passing activities or events are those things that pass, not things you live your life by. However, take pride, do even small things with style.

Creation is now, nurturing is now, as are affirmations, chants, mantras and prayers. Always pay attention to, and affirm, and validate now. **This now shift is how you get there, and, be there, from here.**

If a tornado is headed right for you, yes, head to the safe corner, all the while thinking, saying and feeling, it's all good!

"Now" is this moment, and moment to moment is how we live our lives. You are creating, recreating and refining your life in this moment bringing next moments.

If something is not going the way you want, the reason may be from the past, so what?! Fix it now! If not now, when? Do it now! Perceive things the way you would be happy to be living them now.

If you would like a "bridge," hope is a good thing. You can think of hope as a bridge to get you to your object and simply pay attention to the object of your hope.

"I hope, as the years go by in our marriage, we continue to experience extraordinary happiness."

"I hope as the children grow, we share more and more good times and love."

Hope works for some people and others require something they say is more concrete. Use whatever words you find useful, and keep your awareness on your objective.

Another point on your music. You have your tune, tone, or notes, and you have your lyrics. Another thing about your music is tempo. Are you easy listening or are you rock and roll? Or both, when one or the other suits you? And rhythm? Are you a steady beat? 1 - 2 - 3 - 4, 1 - 2 - 3 - 4, 1 - 2 - 3 - 4, or is your music like a heart beat? How do you feel about the 1 - 2 - 3, 1 - 2 - 3, 1 - 2 - 3 of a waltz?

This is for fun to give you ideas of how you can create your music to enhance and affect your mood and your life.

If you are lucky enough to feel fear, excitement, or anxious about something, consider yourself blessed and make sure your energy is feeding what you want fed. Feeding is manifesting.

These more intense emotions are your magnificent resource if focused on the right stuff.

Fear is a great thing and it's just another word for some kind of perhaps intense emotion. Use fear well by focusing it on your desired objects.

These emotions, however you want to label them, are just energy. Energy does not care how you label it. Electricity comes out of the wall just the same for opera, Enya, or rock and roll.

Labeling may be the ego and drama or it may just be the information. Get past your ego and this is all very, very simple.

What is your favorite song?

Chapter 5
See, Hear, Feel, Describe

"Ask, and it shall be given you; seek, and you shall find; knock, and it shall be opened to you."[5]

– Luke 11:9 (KJV)

What we want is a reliable fast way to attract the good things we are interested in experiencing, and keep the good we have. The success of this hinges on the "story" we tell ourselves about reality and its congruency.

The way to attract and maintain is a function of what our energy is on.

So, we focus our energy. How do we focus? We describe. The description is the story. The description is the bull's eye.

Consider the universe as one big shopping complex, the

Mall of Galaxies. And you live on a planet in the mall complex. Your planet Earth happens to be 75% water. So, what do you think? You think boat.

The Mall of the Galaxies is very accommodating. It will give you anything. But, do not just ask for a boat. Generality is not your friend in this instance. You say, "I like boat!" The mall sends you what, a toy boat, a canoe, a photo, a model boat?

Specifics and you'll do better. "I like a 67 foot Lagoon, catamaran sailboat with this and that. I am willing to go a little larger and I can be very happy in the near 50 foot if it's decked out right."

Or, "I can feel good anytime with a fishing boat in my life. I really like the one with the big Mercs on the back and the foot control troll motor so I can stand up on the bow and concentrate on my casting."

The point is, the universe, the infinite Is, is always responding, paying attention, as it were, to you constantly, and your description of things, and how much and what type of energy you give these things of your focus or contemplation. This life force, matching your vibration, is constantly at work. It never sleeps! It is pure creation.

The basics are again simple. You can describe what a thing, a situation, or condition looks like, sounds like, feels like, smells like, tastes like.

See, Hear, Feel, Describe

The basic description includes features.

All of your describing, which includes your reasoning, involves your five senses. Maybe not all at once, but the more the better.

Ideally we will see a pretty picture, meaning a desirable image, have good words going through our head, and feel good about what we see and hear and, feel the delightful reality of living these visions and stories.

The way we perceive the world is the way we will communicate the world.

The way we perceive our world is the way we represent our world, in the sense of re-present! Our perception is followed by our description.

What follows in this chapter are the basics of all communication. These basics, you will discover, are what you use, and where you come from, in all communication in all areas of your life!

All you add is enthusiasm. This is really very simple, as you will soon discover.

The foundation components of our objective, happiness, are clarity and congruence. We want our feelings, talk, actions and pictures to match.

The story I tell myself about what my reality is, and

the way I want to live my life, is of utmost importance. It's what I believe and where the energy is!

We use mental clarity and fine-tuned emotions to successfully attract that which we desire!

Because we perceive the world around us through our senses, from our senses we will build the story we say is reality for us.

We see, hear, touch, taste, and smell our world. We have our five senses plus intuition. Intuition for some of us is direct knowing. People tend to have a favorite sense in perceiving and communicating their world.

The three favorites seem to be sight, sound and touch. These sensory preferences are also known as visual, auditory, and kinesthetic.

In communication, people will let you know what their favorites are by the words they choose. Let's explore what may be your favorites? Do you have a favorite? Are you using the whole see, hear, feel sensory alphabet?

For example when people meet:
"Nice to **see** you."
"Good to **talk** with you."
"I am glad to be in **touch** with you."
and,
"See you later."

> **"Talk** to you soon."
> "Let's be in **contact**."

and,

> "I **see** what you mean."
> "I **hear** what you're saying."
> "I **grasp** your meaning."

In the example communications note the sensory refer-ences in bold. Reference to a sense simply indicates a possible preference. This is nothing important in and of itself, simply a preference.

Many of us seem to have a favorite and a backup to our favorite. In our order of favorites, the third should be as comfortable as the rest. Being balanced or equally strong in the three is desirable.

If you are equally at home in visual, auditory and kines-thetic, you have more resource available in communica-tion, both with yourself and others. See what I mean? Hear what I'm saying? Got the feel for it?

Your internal and external preferences may match, they may not. That is up to you.

How You Describe Things is Up to Only You

Variables are worth noting. At work or in school you may be quite the auditory person. On vacation perhaps visual or perhaps kinesthetic is your preference. At home you may prefer kinesthetic. Which serves you better when and where? These are your personal choices.

If a man is a kinesthetic slob at home, only interested in his comfort and his wife prefers visual order, meaning clean, the vision of his comfort may be unbearable for her.

What if he is auditory all day at the office and when he comes home he does not want anything to do with words or numbers, he just wants to go for a walk while she wants to exchange stories about her day and his day?

The point worth noting is that communication can go wrong or right depending on your awareness of another's sensory preferences. If you can be comfortable in all three, then you have all three as resource.

When you identify and respect another's preference, understanding is better, communication is better, life is better.

In a simply organized person all these things cross reference and balance. We see a world around us, we hear the sounds, we walk on it, sit on it, and live our life on it.

The eyes will be looking up if one is visualizing or seeing something in their mind's eye. Left or right level eye movement indicates auditory referencing and looking down indicates kinesthetic or feelings being accessed.

Tone of voice up higher might indicate a picture with the words or just a visual preference while talking. Tone of voice down lower may indicate warmth or comfort.

In the kinesthetic, a person might talk with their hands high, medium or low, fast or slow. Sometimes over-weight people tend to be kinesthetic. The white race has tendencies; the black race has tendencies. We all have tendencies. A tendency is where we are comfort-able.

Pay attention to these aspects of life in yourself and others. In doing so, you will better understand yourself, how to successfully communicate with others, and describe life.

A first choice in interaction of any nature is safety. The question is, is this person, place, or thing, friend or foe, adversarial or friendly? Hopefully we learn to pay atten-tion and successfully sort out what is friendly and what might be a threat. Am I safe or not safe? Do I feel good about this, whatever it is?

If visual is your strong preference, then you are going to feel better with others who have that same visual prefer-ence.

Those with auditory preference are going to be more comfortable with other talkers.

A kinesthetic may not be able to "see" what another is

"saying" and still have a good "feel" for whatever is the communication!

Kinesthetic preference people might seem psychic, after all, words and pictures seem a very small part of their communication. Visual or auditory may be their back-up or the same may be out of their conscious awareness.

This sensory reference is all we have and you can be equally balanced in the main three. Awareness in this sensory reference aspect of life and communication is of great value in your applications of congruence in the story you tell yourself about life and what's up.

When you identify another's sensory preference in their communication, respect them their choice, and communicate back to them using their preference, you have a friend.

Chapter 6
Cornerstone of the Mechanics
Intention

*"Learn what the magician knows
and it's not magic anymore."*[6]

— Richard Bach

You have desires. There are many things you wish to experience. This includes things to have and do and be. When you can clearly identify and describe these things, they come to you more quickly. See, write, say, and feel your desires.

The following is a formula to help you understand what you can do in this creation of the life you would be happy with, a creation formula.

intent (x) mechanism (=) result

In a nutshell, have absolutely clear intention; that clear intention will equal your result.

Your intention is what you would be, do or have.

The mechanism is you and the universe in partnership in the creation and manifestation of your intention.

The result is the result.

Some aspects in the mechanics of this creation will be done by you and seen by you. Much activity will be unseen by you and outside your awareness.

"The moment one definitely commits oneself, then providence moves too... A whole stream of events issues from the decision, raising in one's favor all manner of unforeseen incidents and meetings and material assistance."

— Goethe

Invisible forces in your partnership will create coincidences. You might meet a person, something will show up, all manner of coincidence and things that seem like miracles will happen around and near you. Again, pay attention. Some things will be obvious while some others will be subtle.

An interesting aspect of this creation stuff is that a useful coincidence may have happened in your life a week before you set your intention. Something may have come into your life years ago which then was useless and now is perfectly pertinent.

Quantum reality will win over space/time reality because it seems to have few particular rules or laws.

Intention and observation are large parts of the creation of reality from the quantum point of view. As the observer of your goals and aspirations you are also the creative participant, influencing result, by virtue of your observation.

Mechanism in this formula is always (1).

However simple or complex your way of going about something is, it is your single (1) way. The universe is infinite in resource and however all of this adds up, the way it happens is the way. Mechanism is always (1).

Even as your way may change and adapt, your result will equal your intention. Do you see that an ambiguous intention, less than 100%, may get less result than desirable result? Be as clear as you can be in your descriptions of your intentions and firm in your resolve.

Description is important. Description is where you have a lot of control over the events in your life, the coming attractions.

100% intention (=) result 100%

Intention is you being quite conscious. This is a state of

being very awake, clear, and purposeful. Thus, you are focussed and confident. You are absolutely clear on and about the result.

I do not mean to imply tension. You can be very awake, alert and relaxed.

Your intention is your design. Your design is the result of your description.

Your acceptance of what you intend must be built into all of this. Your acceptance is having the room and the time for the thing you are allowing into your life. Make room for things to happen.

Keep up your conscious interest. Paying attention yet again, a worthwhile question is, will you be able to easily enhance, alter what you have manifested, or get rid of it?

Back to our formula, Intent x Mechanism = result.

Intention is more than a state of mind. It is more a complete state of being, which includes emotion, thought, spirit and activity.

For faster results, and more fun, be conscious of the spirit of your intention, how good you can feel about it, and your unwavering focus, which is to mean your conviction. Have absolute confidence you can enjoy the result.

If your intention is 100%, your result will be 100%. Whatever you need for purposes of mechanism will come to you. Have the faith.

Keep your eyes and ears open for opportunities related to your intent. You have no idea when the universe or providence will present something for the attainment of your goal.

Let's spend a moment on the style of your intent. What you read now belongs in a strategies chapter, but it fits so well here, let's go with it.

You may notice Be Do Have showing up here and there in these pages. Each of these is a state. There is the state of being something, the state of doing something and the state of having. Each state is experience.

These three have been labeled a model of life. You can be, then do and have; you can also have, then do and be.

Let's clarify this with the example of a person who would be a drummer. A person need not have a drum set. A person need not even have lessons at first. If the person is in the state of mind of a drummer, she or he can grab a pair of wooden spoons and start on a bucket. Then do the lessons and at some point have the bongos or the drum set. This is an example of the Be Do Have strategy.

An example of the other way around is a parent buys a drum set and their child comes home to it one afternoon completely surprised and does the lessons because Mom and Dad set them up, and becomes a drummer. This is an example of the Have Do Be strategy.

Which strategy makes more sense? Aside from the obvious waste of time if the child is not interested, attempting to put the energy from without to within can be like attempting to put the bean plant back into the seed. But, having and experiencing things can light the spark of creativity developing genius.

Be Do Have is a natural flow in the creation of things; Have Do Be is not. Essence precedes being.

My drum instructor would not let me have more than a pair of sticks and a practice pad for many months because he wanted me to focus on drumming, being a drummer, not all the stuff.

The practical aspect of this is, if you can Be in a state of mind, Do the behaviors, and Have attitudes that relate to the life you wish to live, your energy towards its creation is powerful.

Having a Porsche is one thing. Being a Porsche driver is another. The question straight to the point is, which is more power regarding life energy? Having power can be big. Being power is huge. Essence is infinite.

This is another key point in our "art of attraction." The point is to come from a state of being in these matters. If you are interested in success, be in the state of mind of success and feel successful. Act and behave like you are a success, now, and have been!

Remember the quote from the Messiah's Handbook, Reminders for the Advanced Soul, by Richard Bach, *"To bring anything into your life, imagine that it's already there."* Perhaps you would state the quote for yourself this way, "To bring anything into my life, I live like it is here now!"

"Here" means with me (you) now!

Having something, whether it's a car you drive or art you enjoy, is part of the power toward creation or maintaining the thing, whether an object, situation or condition. Condition, of course, includes states of mind and beingness.

Being the driver, being the connoisseur, is a much more powerful state than wanting or having. Make the things you desire into a state of being. Being is life.

The least power is in "Have", the having of things. More power is inherent in "Do", the doing of things. The maximum power is in "Be". The complete package is to Be and Do and Have. And to this add the practice of gratitude with appreciation and live a very rich life!

So, from a strategic standpoint, in living the life you wish to live, practice being who, what, when, where, and how you want to Be. Think about this and understand that the ramifications are multidimensional.

Now back to intent. You have your intent and your mechanism. The universe, or God, or the Is knows only success. If the Universal could be said to have intent, the intent would only be fulfillment. The mechanism is infinite. Additionally, no matter whatever paradise you can imagine, infinite Providence can do better for you.

You have no idea the extent of miracles, coincidences, blessings, surprises, shifts, and what-have-you that will happen for you, or have already happened, in your practice of the art of attraction and creation.

"Imagine the universe as beautiful and just and perfect. Then be sure of one thing: The Is has imagined it quite a bit better than you have."

Messiah's Hand Book, Illusions,
The Adventures of a Reluctant Messiah
— Richard Bach

So, you must keep your eyes and ears open because useful things are always showing up. You have to know what these might be. The useful thing could be anything, a contact person, advertisement, something in the mail, some person mentions something, a wrong turn that takes you to a right place, anything. This is the infinite game.

Something may show up in-your-face, something else may be quite subtle. Some necessary answer may have been nearby since last week. A friend may "notice something and pass it on to you," having no idea the value. You must pay attention. Our "Is" knows no bounds. None!

Results and Timing

Consider a bean seed in good dirt three inches under the surface in springtime. Energy from the sun gets into the ground to the seed which has potential. Moisture joins and things start happening.

The speed at which things develop depends on quality of dirt, depth of the seed, amount of sun and moisture. Please note that while you are observing the surface, your eyes see none of the development within the seed or underground.

Then one day you see a sprout! What was going on first was the development of roots, followed by the beanstalk and tiny leaves, then more stalk growth, branches and leaves, and finally beans.

The point here to be aware of is, you plant a seed with a decision and your intention, backed up with your resolve. If you have made a good quality decision with conscious intention and firm resolve, you have placed a good "seed" in good "ground" and the universal creation force will have begun the development.

Further note that as with our plant, you will not see everything going on in the development. We can name this first part in the process of manifestation, the subjective development, which is on the way to objective reality, development and fruition.

The timing from the germination to the manifestation is going to have lot to do with your stories, meaning your internal dialogue. The stories you tell yourself about life being difficult or easy, never having enough or always having excess, are key.

Your story telling has quality and quantity aspects. For instance, if you have a clear, well-defined description that makes you happy and a drone of how rotten your life usually is, remember the universe is listening to everything. We hope that quality always wins over quantity, but what might be the time involved in your desired victory?

We want quality to win over quantity, even as we drive by the steak house on our way to fast food burgers. Pay attention to habits, autopilot is not necessarily your best friend. Again, it's that pay attention thing.

When you have your high quality intention, know that development is underway. Belief now is a real good strategy, knowing is better. Be careful with doubt or what might be termed negativity. Doubt will neutralize. Be confident! Now is the moment of creation.

If you fear the outcome, that's energy to the project. By the way, is that fear or excitement you're feeling? The fear, if that's what you wish to label that feeling, is very useful. Just do not let doubt and such change your outcome picture.

Energy and outcome — that's the whole game!

When people ask why things seem to be slow, I say consider the roots, the roots are in development! Something is going on subjectively. (And by the way, did you hear or notice energy on "slow" in that question?)

Remember, faith in the amount of the size of a mustard seed is all it takes. Not a wavering faith, a true faith. Faith defined as complete trust or confidence.

Chapter 7
The Soup

"The aphorism, 'As a man thinketh in his heart so is he,' not only embraces the whole of a man's being, but is so comprehensive as to reach out to every condition and circumstance of his life."[7]

— James Allen

In chapter three you were introduced to personal energy. Personal energy is what you have direct control over. You can generate it, focus it, direct it, and dispel it, among other things.

Now let's explore a larger energy, the infinite energy which Deepak Choprah refers to as "pure potentiality." This energy is infinite and it is what the law of attraction people refer to as "the universe." This infinite source of vibration is that which becomes everything.

The vibrational energy you generate is from and part of the universal energy.

This universal energy, this pure potential, has one job and that is increase. What this means, to you and I, is increase of our individual energy and what it is focused on, the objects of our thoughts and feelings. It knows not time or space, fact nor fiction, or what's good or bad. It responds to you moment to moment, the objects of your focus, and matches the quality of your energy and increases it.

The "law" of attraction is that the universe or universal energy must and can, only match you vibration for vibration. The "art" of attraction is in doing what you want with what you know about creating and directing energy.

In your imagination let's sit out on a bench beside a path for a moment. Here we are in a glorious warm morning. Clouds drift by in the mid morning summer sky and we listen to the leaves rustle on the trees.

We hear the sound of the leaves with the sound of the breeze. We see the leaves move, but we do not see the wind.

The wind is invisible, as is the air. The force which moves the air is invisible. The force that moves that force is invisible. Finer and finer forces, subtle and more subtle forces behind this and all things.

The Soup

A thought, a feeling, or an intention can start movement. Manifestation as physical or experienced reality begins somewhere as the finest of energies.

There is a force, a subtle substance, with which we are surrounded and with which we are permeated. We might as well call it "life." My nickname for it is the "soup." It is a life force, a life source, and re-source. It is the original source, the source of all that is, has ever been or ever will be. Life source / life force / life energy. It is substance, and energy and potential. It is where everything comes from. It is where everything is. It is vibratory. It is vibration. It is frequency.

It is every thing, every where, every when. It is music, magnetism, rivers, and rocks. It permeates everything in varying densities. It is you.

"We must assume behind this force the existence of a conscious and intelligent Mind."
— Max Planck, father of quantum theory

You and I (and everyone) are all bio-magnets. We have the ability to attract, repel, direct and redirect and do so either unconsciously or deliberately.

The life force will guide you, control your actions, and respond to your commands.

God is said to be omnipresent, omniscient, and omnipotent. Omnipresent is everywhere. Omniscient is all knowing. Omnipotent is all powerful. And so is true with our life force.

On a gross level you and I are 98.6 degree furnaces (37C). Fuel in, heat is created, and waste out. We eat, food calories are turned into heat calories, and we go to the toilet. Up a level or so this furnace has legs and feet, arms and hands. This body of ours can move about. Up another level and there is a lot more going on with this feeling thinking expression of life which is you.

On a higher level yet you are a bio-magnetic vibrational co-creator with God. By the way, any ground you walk upon is holy ground.

As a living magnet, you attract, and things are created in and around you, matching your energy and your focus. Your choice of focus comes into play because you are a creature of free will. And remember "around you" is a pretty big place, so is within.

The "I am" that is you, is the seed and the flower of all you are.

This life energy moves, or flows, in infinite rivers and ocean like currents, and quite multi-dimensionally.

The life energy is responsive and like the electricity available in your wall outlets, it will make beautiful music for you or horror stories as you choose with your attention.

The Soup

An infinite supply of power and intelligence is available to you all the time. No lamp to rub. No genie. No limit.

Here is the very good news and the very bad news all in one sentence. This life energy intelligence is "listening" and responding to you more constantly and with more consistency than every beat of your heart. No escape!

By virtue of the fact that you exist and are conscious, you are creating, re-creating and/or sustaining your life experiences, consciously and subconsciously, in all manner all the time.

Your degree of participation and influence in the conditions your life is your decision! Your influence is one hundred percent, which includes the power to give up control. If you find you have inadvertently lost some control over your life, take it back.

"We get results in exact accordance with our understanding of the law and our ability to make proper application."
The Master Key System
– Charles F. Haanel

When you hear someone comment about this kind of philosophy being bogus, such as, bad things happen to people all the time, or we only have a little control, we are victims of fate, etc., remember what you know about the universe "listening", matching, and giving them exactly what they expect... the story they tell themselves.

The Objective is Happiness

"Argue for your limitations and they are yours."
Messiahs Handbook, Reminders for the Advanced Soul
(The Lost Book from Illusions)
— Richard Bach

Your salvation or safety net is to be grateful always. Have a state of mind and feelings of gratitude. Practice gratitude with every possible opportunity! Right along with your gratitude be happy, then you'll be safe to play with intention. Gratitude and happiness will cover or fix accidental errors and slips in intention.

In continually practicing gratitude, you are creating more and more things to be grateful for.

Remember, if "now" is what you have, and you are creating and/or sustaining and attracting what your energy is on, your energy should be "on" the best, biggest, new and improved, most rewarding items you can possibly conceive, believe or wonder about and be happy about.

Negative thoughts have no chance at manifestation if you live happily and are grateful at all times. The weeding in your garden of life becomes automatic.

Your energy will only be creating a life congruent and consistent with being happy and grateful. Those two are your basics. Also be clever, giving, creative, loving, and interested.

So, what are you going to do? ...or be or have?

Chapter 8
State of Mind & Awe

Darla: *"Alfalfa, will you swing me before we have lunch?"*
Alfalfa: *"Sure Darla."*
Spanky: *"Say Romeo, what about your promise to the he-man
      woman hater's club?"*
Alfalfa: *"I'm sorry Spanky, I have to live my own life."*[8]

— Spanky and Our Gang

Awe and Gratitude

This thing we call life, this glorious adventure, is remarkable. Remarkable in simplicity and equally remarkable in complexity.

Two words worth your time and study to completeness are gratitude and awe. Let's start with awe. You expand on it and apply it to gratitude. Awe, and awesome, is what is stunning, profound, magnificent, inspiring, wondrous and more. In your study, feel the feeling of awe and remember, if that's the energy you are experiencing, that is the energy you are spreading, your world will vibrate and manifest back to you in kind.

Consider the energy you develop and put out when you are in a state of awe. A state of true awe is the greatest state. You feel truly alive!

Start with noting something that astounds you and explore this amazement and multiply it.

I am absolutely in awe of everything in my life.

I am in awe that the dog, cats, chickens and peacocks all get along.

I am in awe of my health.

I am in awe of the love of my life! So many improbable aspects and not a problem anywhere.

I am in awe of what happens with people when I teach, coach, and do the seminar trainings. I am in awe when out walking in the city or nature.

Take nature, how can a feeling thinking person not be in awe of a plum blossom and the fragrance? The cynic might say, yeah, I know, but it's just there so the insects are attracted and pollination happens for the continuation of the insect species, etc.

Then again... why do I get to smell this beautiful fragrance which for me is only pleasure? There are probably many bug things I cannot smell. Why does this beautiful thing happen for me to enjoy? And that is just one sensation to enjoy from nature. Nature has sights, sounds, smells, tastes and textures. 10,000 sensations for our happiness. Awesome!

Take a look at the back of your hand. What you may not see right away is the blood pulsing and simultaneously carrying nutrients, oxygen on half its journeys through and around your body and on the remainder of the journeys still carrying nutrients, carbon dioxide and waste.

I use the plural journeys because there are so many things beginning, ending, and going on simultaneously. A journey could be said to begin at your heart, another your lungs, and then there's the kidneys, liver and all of this goes on in your one bloodstream at the same time. Awesome!

Another book for you to write and put on your bookshelf of life is, *Where I Have Found Awe*.

Joy is a state of happiness, which certainly weaves well with awe. Other words which express feelings similar to joy are merriment, delight, glee, gaiety, and our old friend, happiness. :-)

And here again is room for gratitude. There's always room for gratitude. Be grateful you can notice things.

Be grateful you can appreciate things. Be grateful you can feel joy. Be grateful you can feel! Be grateful for basics and simplicity.

In a brief look into gratitude what is the object of your gratitude? Do you appreciate the object of your gratitude? How much do you appreciate the object of your gratitude? The good feelings are of what nature?

Two of the most powerful forces in creation are awe and gratitude.

Gratitude

In this diagram the heart represents the object of your gratitude. The infinity path represents the ever circulating energy of your thoughts and feelings for the object of your gratitude.

Awe and gratitude are two very high powerful forms of energy.

Here may be your grandest exercise. Get into a state of mind which is that of awe, gratitude, and delight. Now do somethng with it. Make your day!

You are free to choose your state of mind.

Chapter 9
Exercises

"Imagination is everything. It is the preview of life's coming attractions."[9]

— Albert Einstein

Yes, there are exercises throughout this book, yet here is this chapter with exercises.

This chapter on exercises is about managing energy. First you may be interested in increasing your own energy, and after that cleaning up character or attitude issues for effective and desirable use of energy.

Start with thinking about the "soup" you read and learned about in chapter seven. Consider that there is this force, this potential which permeates all life. What meaning does this potential have for you? What are its attributes?

In your contemplation of this life force, wonder how powerful it is and you will start to become more and more aware of it as your connection with life's force becomes stronger and your personal power increases.

The warm-up exercise is to wonder about this soup, so think about it, have feelings about it, consider the strength of your partnership with it, and it will increase within you. Do this exercise 30 minutes twice a day.

In your exploration consider the basics like respect, love, and happiness, plus important things particular to you.

Remember, this life force energy matches you.

Another warm-up exercise of this nature is to breathe this life force consciously. As part of your usual breathing in and out your nose, consider or imagine that you are breathing in this life force, and as you fill your lungs with air, you fill every cell in your body from your head to your toes with the life energy.

Good times to do this are sunrise, in the rain, and right after a rain or thunderstorm, and anytime you think of it. Add this dimension to your breathing and many things to do with your health and well-being will improve. What makes the difference is your consciousness, meaning how you pay attention!

The practice of gratitude is exercise number one of

another sort. Develop a very long and true list of things for which you are grateful! Practice laughing. Find things to laugh about. Laughter is your second exercise, of this sort, followed by giving, focus, and three more for change and improving life.

Whatever you are doing, give it all your attention. What ever you look at or listen to, look sharp and listen well. Focus is a rewarding exercise!

Your intention in each exercise is important.

Exercise One

Be grateful. Feel gratitude. Express gratitude. Study and consider gratitude. Write that book mentioned earlier in chapter three. Write the journal of everything you are grateful for. Explore the various ways you can express gratitude and write them in your journal.

As you get into bed to sleep, get out of bed and start paying attention to go through your day, think or say, "thank you," about everything and anything you can possibly appreciate.

Use wonder and awe to fuel your gratitude with feelings of how awesome and wonderful life can be!

You will get to a state of feeling so grateful for so much you will have a huge flow of things to be grateful for coming to you constantly.

Exercise Two

Laugh.

You must have heard somewhere in your life, laughter is the best medicine. Practice and develop a sense of humor. The higher quality energy is in clever lighter humor. Study types and styles of humor.

"You've got to learn to laugh, it's the way to true love."
— John Travolta as Michael in
the motion picture *Michael*

Exercise Three

Give. Give of yourself. Give respect. Give to yourself. Give to others. Give consideration. Give a smile. Give money. Give of your talents. Give a nod of your head. Give appreciation. Give creatively.

To paraphrase something important on giving by Deepak Chopra in his book, *The Seven Spiritual Laws of Success*, your intention in giving is what is most impor-tant. Your intention should include happiness for both the giver and receiver and, he goes on to say, happiness is life-supporting and therefore generates increase.

Consider all the many simple ways we all can give which return so much. Write this list! Use yourself as a point of reference. For example, do you like to be appreci-ated, then express appreciation to others.

Exercise Four

Focus. Pay attention to what you focus on moment to moment. What do you focus on in the specialty areas of your life, like grocery shopping, holidays, vacations, your work and recreation?

What do you pay attention to in your immediate vicinity? What do you focus on regarding your future? How do you pay attention to your physical health? How much attention do you give your spiritual health? What should you give more attention to? Where are you scattered and where are you ahead of the game? What is easy for you to pay attention to? Have fun with this list and be honest.

Here next are two of the best process exercises.

Exercise Five

Your hands and change.

An interesting thing that works one hundred percent of the time is putting the worst and the best together and the best always comes out on top.

The process will make more sense as we get right into the exercise. What you need here is simply some good news and some bad news, or any news you'd like to be better, a piece of paper and something with which to write.

For example, my car is a mess; I'd like to feel good about my clean car. How about, I feel miserable versus, I prefer feeling fit and energetic? Or, there are these sarcastic people around me and I'd rather be treated with respect.

Based on these examples, note you can change your priorities, your state of mind, and interaction with others. Your intent is important and no one loses. Where others may be involved, they win also.

The first part of this exercise is done on paper where you write the less than desirable aspects on the left side only. This left side is the something you wish to change completely or for the better. The right side of the paper will be the good news, the desirable outcome! This is only because we read and write from left to right, from past into future.

Be creative if you wish by using colored pencils, lipstick, paint or whatever. Give yourself plenty of room to mark it up.

By the way, give yourself enough time for the exercise, something like 20 to 90 minutes. You can also work on this on and off for a few days or a week at the most.

For everything on the left side of your page, have the relative desirable counterpart, the resolution, on the right side. Study your page. When you are clear on what is changing or improving, draw a line through or cross out the less than desirable, item by item, and underline or color up the desirable items.

Study your page and what you've done. Congratulations, you've done the exercise!

You could burn this paper or frame it. I keep mine around sometimes until I lose them or one day just pitch them. I keep them for a while for possible review. I always smile when I review.

Wait a second, you may want to save that paper to add an additional dimension to exercise five with exercise six next.

Exercise Six

In the second part of the exercise you will, with your imagination, imagine these aspects of the bad news in the palm of perhaps your left hand. Then, all the very good news aspects or the resolution to "X" in your other hand.

Let's make the hand you write with your future hand, if that's all right. Good news aspects will then be imagined on the palm of this future hand after the less than desirable is imagined on your other palm.

Ok, now one hand at a time. The less than desirable first. Hold your palm up and imagine the colors, shapes, sounds, and textures being on that palm. What are the colors associated with X? If the colors need to be drab, make them so. The sounds may be screechy or whatever, the textures slimy or harsh, and the smells and the tastes bad. Go ahead with your imagination, this is only temporary.

Not everything has to be drama, but if you have the opportunity and drama seems useful, use it.

That hand should be becoming somewhat heavy.

Begin to load your other palm with the desirables. The colors will be more pleasing as will the sounds, textures, fragrances and taste if you're using taste.

If you can work in happiness, respect, confidence and validation on this side, please do!

After we have developed each of the news's on paper and we have transferred and developed each on its palm, we will establish that the less-than-desirable hand is heavy and might smell really bad etc., while the desirable side is light, delightful, and smells really great.

Holding your hands, palm up, in front of you you may feel an apparent weight difference. Relax a moment... and now we finish it up.

Here you are with both palms face up in front of you, one heavy, one light. You know what is represented in the palm of each hand. Open your eyes if they have been closed, begin to spread your arms and clap your hands together with good slap sound and mush the two news's together. Really mix them up well, kind of like they were the consistency of soft clay or cookie dough.

Then when you have all this thoroughly mixed, hold your hands clasped, feel the energy, and open your hands slowly like a flower blossoming. Smell with your imagination a beautiful fragrance, look and see colors like the richest translucent rainbow you've ever seen, hear sounds that bring an emotional welling up in you, and notice how good and clean, fresh and light you feel. You may have a vision such as an alpine meadow in your mind. Your choice. Stay with this good feeling for a time.

To respect and validate what you have done, do something. The something could be take a walk, some small celebration, simply take a shower, or have a candle light bubble bath.

That completes the exercise.

Practice this exercise and you will get so good at it you will bring tears to your eyes and feelings of great happiness. It can be done in a minute.

Now that you know the structure of the exercise please be clear that the integration of all five of your senses is extremely beneficial if you can put them all into play.

If a picture is worth a thousand words, use pictures. Use black and white, use color, make them 3-D, make them moving pictures.

For the sound part use words, sounds and maybe music. You can hear and see words. Can you hear happy sounds on that future side? Laughter? Complements? Praise?

Pay attention to feelings of tension, weakness, strength, and what have you.

You have had experiences of things that taste or smell one way or another and you can remember.

That's it! Review if you feel so inclined. You are ready to do it again and again.

Exercise Seven

Let's take a lesson from the pros! Action! Grab a pencil. You are about to become your own life movie producer. You create this movie to give life to your desires.

If a picture is worth a thousand words and we can make it color and give it texture, what is a moving picture with you in it worth in words?

What you will do here is write a story. Use the setting you want with the lighting you want, and sounds and whatever effects you wish.

Exercises

This is going to take more than a sheet of paper. Write what your objective is. The objective is that happiness you wish most to live.

What is your happiness? A vocation? A relationship? Perhaps an adventure? You can have what you want, just start somewhere.

This happiness could be a person, place or thing, a situation or condition. You pick what it is for you. The usual suspects are money, fitness, job, mate, purpose and, you know best.

You set the stage and you are the director. Watch what you wish for, it might just come true.

Now write your details. This will be a movie you will run over and over in your mind.

In your details include the back ground or setting, rich colors, sounds including conversations, music, sounds of nature, babbling brook, birds. If your setting has trees maybe you can hear the leaves and wind chimes.

Nature does not have to have anything to do with your production. Perhaps your setting is the entire top floor of a high-rise in the city of your dreams over looking a river. And there I go throwing nature into the mix again. This is your creation!

Write it as if it were an entire world. Development of your

inner neighborhood is part of what may be going on with this exercise. You have an infinite amount of room or space in your inner neighborhood.

You are the primary developer, and in the development of your dreams and goals the buddy system works. Involve a friend if you like. Make it a happy ending.

This exercise is good for your state of mind and your health. Any good state of mind is good for your health.

These exercises all exist to accomplish one or two things, the adjustment of your state of mind and your focus.

The constant exercise for you is your practice of gratitude. Feel grateful for all you have, are able to do and are. Acknowledge what you have created, desirable or not. Acknowledgment is validation. Validation is power.

Respect and validate yourself in all things!

Chapter 10
Strategies

"All people climb the same mountain. The mountain, however, has many pathways – each with a different view. A person knows and understands only what he sees from his own pathway, and as he moves, his view will change. Only when he reaches the top of the mountain will he see and understand all the views of mankind..."[10]

— Pali Jae Lee and Koko Willis

Strategies and a little more on inner world

If you are going to "want," you must know where you're coming from.

The statement, "I want (*whatever*)," is an interesting study in energy. If a person is coming from a place of "I do not have" in the sense of lack, then the energy is "I lack (*whatever*)." Another person who is used to having whatever they want is making, or having, an energy such as, "Yup, (*whatever*) is what is next in my life!"

Belief, confidence, expectation and such should be behind all wants, wishes and desires which you would truly have in your life!

Wanting too intensely may become an affirmation of, "I don't have...!" Now you know the solution is to believe you have received and act accordingly.

Remember what you have learned, change the "I want..." to "I have..."

Consider and know the basis of your energy. Fundamentally you are a winner! You *are* winning. Where are you coming from?

Remember again, now is your moment of creation and your energy of now is the creator of future events, the coming attractions in your life. You are creating!

Also remember, this force or soup of pure potentiality is literal. While it is full of surprises, it is specifically purely literal.

Remember your anticipation of gift giving and receiving as a child? You were in anticipation of what magnificent treasures your gifts would be, and the anticipation of how the gifts you gave would be received. Anticipation, another way of saying expectation, is good energy.

Strategies

First and foremost in strategy is pay attention. Pay attention to yourself, particularly your gut feelings and inner dialogue. Of course, pay attention to things around you. The things of your outer world reflect your inner world. So, be cheerful, creative, patient, respectful and trust.

Your strategies may come from having things, doing things, or being things. You make the evaluation of what your basis is, where you come from in regard to your intention.

You are the one to determine where energy may be easy, or maximum, or leveraged.

In our Be Do Have model balance is good. Being and doing, or doing then being are great starting strategies.

Keep moving and resting and moving, and paying attention, and always be grateful.

Chapter 11
Perspectives & Accountability

"By believing passionately in something that still does not exist, we create it. The nonexistence is whatever we have not sufficiently desired."[11]

— Nikos Kazantzakis

Perspectives

A life force permeates everything everywhere always. Like fish are in water, you and I are in this life force. You may be able to ignore it, but you cannot get away from it. It is in you.

In your body you have 80 - 100 trillion cells, including bone, muscle, tissue, organ, skin, and hair, which are all living, growing, dividing, dying and... when is the last time you told a cell to do anything for you? This is only one aspect of your life force.

The Objective is Happiness

All of us seem to have basic characteristics. A person who is a fighter by nature may be constantly setting up their life for conflicts and challenges to be overcome. A nurturer may set up his or her life to be constantly finding people to save.

Now walk out into a forest and attempt to comprehend all that goes on with the life force.

God may have a plan for you. And then there is this thing called choice.

"Say you can, say you can't, either way you're right."
— Henry Ford

When you have a clear or serious intention, the Is, which is the God force, the all-knowing, knows more than you, sees more than you, and makes things happen according to your intention.

Your main job is intention. So, pay attention! You will be guided.

By shear default you are operating from intention. Some people wave wands, some people point, some hold the interesting desire in their mind's eye and tell no one.

Remember, if you have an intention, the all-knowing "God" force knows infinite ways to make things happen. So, pay attention and act accordingly.

When I write, "pay attention" and "act accordingly," be aware, be alert to things showing up in your life. This may be in your immediate proximity on the same day, or through someone you just met a week later. Your necessary new connection may be someone you met last week!

Be ready to be quite surprised and amazed at how things come together.

By the way, many things written here are just a reminder. You know these things. There may be the turn of a phrase, but the basics are the basics.

If someone says it cannot be quantified, let's have that argument. For good reason the argument must allow coincidence. We simply have too many "random" acts of "things" of "coincidence" coming "together" to discount the notion that there must be some kind of "magic" around "intention!"

Accountability

The main premise here is you are running your own show. And ultimately whether you want to or not, you are. It is that choice thing.

On one end of this accountability scale is the victim and on the other the sovereign.

Victim defined as someone who is more or less controlled by forces outside themselves. Sovereign defined from the Latin super, as above. So, above victimness.

Our religions, schools, groups and clubs we join, all tell us what to focus on and how to feel about it.

On the high end you author your life, you are the authority. Authority as defined from the Latin auctoritus, from auctor, originator.

The stories you tell yourself are what come true. The circumstances are nonfiction.

If you believe you are in some small percentage of control of your life, and mostly circumstances and others control your life, then that will be what is. You are getting what your energy is on.

What matters is how you feel about yourself and how you feel about life! Then operate from a Saturday morning state of mind, a happy clutter free state of mind.

"What this power is, I cannot say. All I know is that it exists and it becomes available only when you are in that state of mind in which you know exactly what you want."
— Alexander Graham Bell

Chapter 12
I am & Affirmations

"For as he thinketh in his heart, so is he."[12]
— King Solomon, Proverbs 23:7 King James

The Nature of Affirmations

An affirmation is a declaration, an assertion, pronounce-ment, pledge and or confirmation among other words. An affirmation is also holding your focus and or holding your position. Commitment is affirmation. Action is affirmation.

When you gaze upon a photograph of you and your loved one you probably generate a feeling. That feeling is an affirmation of the manifestation of a desire. It is confirmation of your continued acceptance.

Most people know affirmations as words, "I am" statements. "I am" statements and affirmations are easily identified as the same thing. Your prayers, meditations and such should all have the qualities of being a complete present moment vision. We are always thinking in the "now." The more clear and steady we are in these moments of "now" the faster our results will be.

The key parts in success of the affirmations working are clarity and room to receive. Do you have room for your visions or a plan to make room? Are you actively working on that plan? Are you fit and ready to live your visions. Here's where allowing comes into play. You must have the mental, emotional, psychological room for the life you wish to live. If you need permission, get it! You may need your own permission; if so, deliberately give yourself the permission.

If you want your soul mate to move in with you, empty half your dressers and closets. Maybe buy a robe (easy sizing) and keep it in the space open for your loved one. And you can be more creative! Books? Small fountain?

I am statements are not the only way to go with verbal affirmations. There are other choices to state ways to be. Here are a couple of examples.

I live the life I wish to live.

I radiate health and well-being.

I maintain my focus.

I am & Affirmations

My attention and focus are superior.

My emotions flow perfectly.

I master my thoughts.

My visions are clear and vibrant.

My health and fitness help me concentrate.

Honor is my foundation.

Being respectful is my nature.

Competence and creativity are mine.

Love surrounds me.

My gratitude brings great reward.

I am Ok!

Affirmations take many forms. Actions are affirmations. Smells, tastes, feelings, listening, watching are affirmations when you treat these as such. Your best affirmation may be joy!

Go for a walk in nature or around the block as an affirmation of your connection with all that is. Sit still peacefilly for a period of time every day as an affirmation of your connection with all that is.

"MY DECLARATION OF SELF-ESTEEM
I AM ME

*In all the world, there is no one else exactly like me
Everything that comes out of me is authentically mine
Because I alone choose it – I own everything about me,
my body, my feelings, my mouth, my voice, all my actions,
whether they belong to others or to myself – I own my
fantasies, my dreams, my hopes, my fears – I own all my
triumphs and successes, all my failures and mistakes –
Because I own all of me, I can become intimately
acquainted with me – By so doing I can love me and be
friendly with me in all my parts – I know there are aspects
about myself that puzzle me, and other aspects that I do not
know — But as long as I am friendly and loving to myself, I
can courageously and hopefully look for solutions to the
puzzles and for ways to find out more about me – However
I look and sound, whatever I say and do, and whatever I
think and feel at a given moment in time is authentically me
– If later some parts of how I looked, sounded, thought and
felt turn out to be unfitting, I can discard that which is
unfitting, keep the rest, and invent something new for that
which I discarded – I can see, hear, feel, think, say, and do
– I have the tools to survive, to be close to others, to be
productive, and to make sense and order out of the world of
people and things outside of me – I own me, and therefore I
can engineer me – I am me and*
I AM OKAY"

Self Esteem, by Virginia Satir

Chapter 13
Review

"Every moment of your life is infinitely creative and the universe is endlessly bountiful. Just put forth a clear enough request, and everything your heart desires must come to you."[13]

— Shakti Gawain

Now that you have a sense of this force and an understanding of how this source as a resource works, you will easily understand the short version of how to improve or change things in and around you.

You must first identify a desire. You must be able to describe what you wish. Creating a clear vision is a powerful description. Think beyond its manifestation or arrival in your life. What will having this desire feel like? How long do you want it?

So, identify what you want rather than what you do not want. Give this desired object attention, mentally, emotionally and in actions. Then make room for it, which is also to say allow it. Allowing lets energy flow!

If you allow, you will get what your energy is on.

The better you can articulate and the more you allow, the faster will be your results.

Pay attention, you will experience surprises. Be open to delightful surprises.

You have three books or journals to write, which were mentioned earlier in these pages:
>   *My Book of Gratitude* (Chapter 3)
>   *How I Pay Attention to Life* (Chapter 3)
>   *Where I Have Found Awe* (Chapter 8)

A fourth book, and equally as much fun, is *My Evidence*. This, of course, is where you write down every instance of result through attraction that you notice. This will become validation. **Validation is the foundation of increase!**

To begin these journals immediately, go to page 111. You will find three pages for each to begin your journaling.

The reminders -
>   You and I are created in the image of God.

I live what my energy is on.
It's already underway.
Feeling is power.
Thought is focus.
Gratitude is powerful.
Awe is powerful.
Allowing is necessary.
Paying attention is worthwhile!
I choose what gives my life meaning!
The game is create and recreate.
Life surrounds us and permeates us.
Now is the important moment.
Be(ing) is the important state.
I've got a name.
I've got a song.
Happiness is the result.
The *Is* knows no bounds
Evidence is validation

Energy is simply energy. How you color energy is the object of your focus and how you feel. You can magnify, choke, or steer it. In these pages we have put our time to focussing, multiplying and redirecting.

You choke and deflect energy when you refuse to allow or doubt. When you allow and help things to happen, energy moves freely and easily. Flow is what we want.

A bottom line very important fundamental is where you come from with your energy.

Is your cup half empty or half full? Are you coming from a place of lack or a place of anticipation? I haven't got it, or, I can feel the joy of it in my life! I wonder how much satisfaction I will experience?

Our infinite source is literal and it will "help" you "want" forever, just as easily as it will help you have and live all your dreams and desires now! If you want what you have, that's a good thing!

I want what I have, is a strong perspective and a powerful place to come from with our energy.

Know your desires, especially how much they mean to you, and allow Divine Providence to deliver.

Chapter 14
Change

"Let a person radically alter his thoughts, and he will be astonished at the rapid transformation it will effect in the material condition of his life."[14]

— James Allen

Change is a good thing. We are all on a journey of changing perspectives, learning new things, trying new things, and discarding here and there.

Life is a flow like a river for some, for others an ocean current, and others the wind.

Consider the impact of making a change. Sometimes just you are involved and many times others and possibly many others are involved by being affected by what you change.

What turned out to be a major change in my life was when I quit smoking after many years of cigarettes. That many years ago. Some of the change I can put into words here. I feel better than ever in my life. A rough calculation and I find I missed out on spending sixty to ninety thousand dollars on butts. No more accidentally burned clothes, furniture, carpet and car seats. No more occasional nights driving to the convenience store because I had to have one. Ashtrays never smelled good. My sense of smell is better for quitting that habit. I do love the smells of plumb blossoms and lilac and new mowed grasses. Anyway, it happened one morning at a breakfast meeting - I quit. I have not smoked since.

I made that decision to stop smoking sitting at the breakfast meeting. I was having my own private conference in my head. "Ok body," I said to myself as I put the last one out, "you can crave, stress me, try to make me crabby and angry. Do your worst! I am putting out my last smoke and that is that." I meant it. I wondered how uncomfortable this quitting might be, but that didn't matter. I was done with it. An interesting thing happened or didn't happen. Nothing happened. I had no cravings and no discomfort. I believe the success was because my resolve was so firm in my mind that whatever in me might have caused any problem, didn't.

To this day I believe if someone makes a decision backed up by firm resolve, the issue is easy.

What would you change in your life?

You read in chapter two the most valuable commodity in life is focus. This focus is the observing or doing of something. Focus certainly is an aspect of paying attention. Another word I like to link with focus is "consider." To focus on something is to consider the thing.

The point is, what is the value of changing focus in your life? This change could be in direction or quality. What do you focus on for joy? A priority list is nothing other than a focus list.

Take small steps. If you change one thing per week for a year that is 52 changes. That's a lot! When you improve one thing every three weeks or three months you are accomplishing a lot over a period of time.

When considering changes, consider the possibilities. Who will be affected? What might be the demands on you, or the relief?

If you go out and buy a horse, do you understand that you just committed yourself to 150 bales of hay, 300 pounds of oats and that's per year, plus a large animal veterinarian, a place to keep it, and the additional time necessary to attend to and enjoy this addition in your life?

You want to be in charge of change in your life wherever possible. Change is flow. Flow is good. We like flow when it is from not so good to good and good to better!

Change is inevitable. Change is going to happen. Resistance may or may not be good use of energy. Changes can sneak up on you, but paying attention will certainly cut the surprises.

Know what you want before someone, or chance, knows it for you!

Make change your friend! ;-)

Epilogue

"You are today where your thoughts have brought you; you will be tomorrow where your thoughts take you."[15]

— James Allen

You have got to pay attention to your thoughts and how much energy you have with them.

This may be the most dangerous book ever written in that this being a true description of the way the universe and life works, you do not want to blow this off by saying it's all bogus and putting any bad attitude energy with that opinion?

If you can no longer claim ignorance, and the force is with you at all times, look up, look out, and pay attention. You are creating.

So I hope you look at some of these concepts and words in new light. Understanding the law of karma is a concept you may be right at home with. Karma is just a word. It represents a powerful concept. And, it is just a word. Then again, as you sew so shall you reap. You are sewing all the time.

Which word works for you, meditation, contemplation, affirmation, focus, chant, mantra, ritual, motivate, affirm, consider, wish, desire, focus, intent, pray? What is your favorite way to direct your energy? The simple lesson is, what are the objects of your intention energy or your consideration? The advanced lesson is, what is the general basic mood or attitude your energy comes from?

I hope you have a better more practical understanding of emotion, the power of emotions, and the power of focus.

A PBS program on the brain says, we are not thinking beings who feel, we are feeling beings who think.

Watch what you energize, it might just come true. Listen to you inner environment and the sounds around you.

Pay attention to what might be the lyrics, your lyrics. What is the music? What is your tone? Make your music what you want it to be. Then, go into your day and have all that you desire. And having the experience of your desires ought to support your happiness, and around and around it goes. One way or another a circle of energy repeating and repeating.

This is your life, and it is probably not just yours. I mean, you have people who love and care about you. That matters. They matter! You matter to them! Your life deserves your respect first.

If you want to talk more later, great! I'll leave you with this for now (author unknown).

"On the sands of hesitation
lie the bones of countless many
who... on the brink of success
sat down to rest,
and resting...

died."

Never give up.

Now get out there, play nice with the other kids!

Recommended Health

Being a human and being more than just a ninety-eight point six (37C) degree furnace requires activity. Things must move. Your blood, heart, and other muscles must move.

Emotions must flow. Blocked emotions may be the number one cause of illness, mental, emotional, and physical.

If you wish to be happy, exercise your sense of humor. If you wish to be brilliant, exercise your creativity. If you wish to be competent, exercise your problem solving abilities. Let these things flow!

We have many types of health, including mental, emotional, physical, spiritual, creative, physical, and more than that. Here are some ideas for that very important conveyance we call our body.

Drink 1/2 ounce of water for each pound you weigh, every day. (Divide your body weight by 2, that number is your ounces to drink.)

- Move -
  - swing your arms
  - walk a couple of times a day
  - jumping jacks
  - tai chi
  - skip, jump rope, rebound
  - swim whenever you can
  - bicycle
  - stretch
- Eat your vegetables.
- Eat your fruits.
- Fish and eggs are good protein.
- Challenge your mind.
- Do not sweat the small stuff.
- Sit for 30 minutes twice a day, do nothing!
- Get good sleep.
- Be as impeccable with your body as you possibly can.
- Be as impeccable with your mind as you possibly can.
- Complete things.
- Simplify your life.
- Be grateful.
- Be happy.

Emotional exercise is easy. It is to laugh and cry with joy or sadness. Blocked emotions are the problem. Anger could be good for cleaning out the pipes so to speak. Have fun with it, just do not break anything or hurt anyone. If your emotions flow freely anger is probably of no concern for you.

Recommended Reading

Here's a short list of some favorites supporting this book. Along with these you can read Newtonian physics, into quantum theory, and related material. Read T. Lobsang Rampa and everything Richard Bach wrote. Supporting material is everywhere if you pay attention.

As a Man Thinketh, James Allen

Awaken the Giant Within, Anthony Robbins

Bible - King James version
          George Lamsa version

Biology of Belief, Bruce H. Lipton M.D.

A Course in Miracles, Dr. Helen Schucman

A Fire from Within, Carlos Casteneda

Illusions, The Adventures of a Reluctant Messiah, Richard Bach

Jonathon Livingston Seagull, Richard Bach

Law of Attraction, The Science of Attracting More of What You Want and Less of What You Don't, Michael Losier

Life and Teaching of the Masters of the Far East, Baird Spalding

The Master Key System, Charles Haanel

Messages from Water, Masaru Emoto

Messiah's Handbook, Reminders for the Advanced Soul, Richard Bach

The Power of Positive Thinking, Norman Vincent Peale

The Power of Intention, Wayne Dyer

Psycho-Cybernetics, Maxwell Maltz

The Seven Spiritual Laws of Success, Deepak Chopra

The Structure of Magic: A Book About Language and Therapy, Richard Bandler

The Structure of Magic II: A Book About Communication and Change, John Grinder

Tao De Jing, by Lao Tze

Recommended Watching

This short list is some favorite motion pictures where I have noticed a gem for life presented in a sentence or a scene that caught my attention and made a lasting difference in my life.

The Astronaut Farmer - advice

Sitting outside the school psychologist's office, Billy Bob Thornton as Charlie Farmer says to the kid on the bench with him, "You better know what you want to do before somebody knows it for you."

Being There - for perspective

This movie is fun in the exercise of simplicity with a wonderful statement on how life works in the last spoken line in the movie. The line comes from over a hill in the distance, "... after all, life is a state of mind."

City Slickers - this has a secret of life

I really dislike these things being termed a secret of life. And at the same time it is a convention many are used to. In this movie the secret shows up midway through with Curly talking to the boys about the secret to life and is completed at the airport near the end of the movie.

The Count of Monte Cristo - fortunes & saints

This one is interesting in several ways. Written originally by Alexandre Dumas who also wrote The Three Musketeers. Edmund Dantez has been wrongfully imprisoned in Chateau Dif for some years and for as many years a fellow prisoner has been digging a tunnel in an unintended direction, which ends up coming up in Edmund's cell and is his rather remarkable fortune.

Field of Dreams - believing and/or trusting

"If you build it they will come," is only part of this motion picture. When you watch this consider what started things, when, and coincidences.

Joe Versus the Volcano - strategy & perspective

This is loaded with symbolism and perspective. I am astounded with what some writers come up with that directors and editors recognize as valuable and is included for the viewing public. Of course, my favorite is the Meg Ryan, as Patricia, quote beginning chapter 1. Another favorite is when Tom Hanks speaks to God with the moon rise.

The Last Samurai - honor and focus

Meet Joe Black - strategy

This loaded with excellent how life should be speeches. Loaded!

MIchael - fun, romance and the art of attraction

Pay it Forward - strategy on giving

Probably the best strategy on abundance Hollywood has produced. This is an attitude and a way of life. The motion picture is from the book, same title, based on a true story.

My Book of Gratitude

I am grateful for -

_____

_____

_____

_____

_____

_____

_____

_____

The Objective is Happiness

My Book of Gratitude

The Objective is Happiness

My Book of Attention

What I like to focus on is -

_____

_____

_____

_____

_____

_____

_____

_____

The Objective is Happiness

_____

_____

_____

_____

_____

_____

_____

_____

_____

_____

_____

_____

My Book of Attention

The Objective is Happiness

My Book of Awe

What amazes me is -

_____

_____

_____

_____

_____

_____

_____

_____

The Objective is Happiness

_____

_____

_____

_____

_____

_____

_____

_____

_____

_____

_____

_____

My Book of Awe

The Objective is Happiness

My Book of Evidence

Here's my proof -

_____

_____

_____

_____

_____

_____

_____

_____

The Objective is Happiness

My Book of Evidence

_____

_____

_____

_____

_____

_____

_____

_____

_____

_____

_____

_____

The Objective is Happiness

Chapter Start Quote Credits

(1)   *"My father says almost the whole world is asleep. Everybody you know, everybody you see, everybody you talk to. He says that only a few people are awake and they live in a state of constant total amazement."* Meg Ryan as Patricia in the movie *joe versus the volcano* produced by AMBLIN ENTERTAINMENT

(2)   *"All that we are is a result of what we have thought."* Buddha, Siddhartha Guatama

(3)   *"Our attitude toward life determines life's attitude toward us."* Earl Nightingale

(4)   *"Within you now and always is the unborn possibility of a limitless experience of inner stability and outer treasure, and yours is the privilege of giving birth to it."* Eric Butterworth

(5)   *"Ask, and it shall be given you; seek, and you shall find; knock, and it shall be opened to you."* Luke 11:9 (King James)

(6)   *"Learn what the magcian knows and it's not magic anymore." Messiah's Handbook, Reminders for the Advanced Soul, The Lost Book from Illusions, Illusions, The Adventures of a Reluctant Messiah*, Richard Bach

(7)   *"The aphorism, 'As a man thinketh in his heart so is he,' not only embraces the whole of a man's being, but is so comprehensive as to reach out to every condition and circumstance of his life."* James Allen

(8)   *Darla:*   *"Alfalfa will you swing me before we have lunch?"*
        Alfalfa: *"Sure Darla."*
        Spanky: *"Say Romeo, what about your promise to the he-man woman hater's club?"*
        Alfalfa: *"I'm sorry Spanky, I have to live my own life." Spanky and Our Gang*, Hal Roach Productions, 1922, (currently MGM)

(9)   *"Imagination is everything. It is the preview of life's coming attractions."* Albert Einstein

(10)   *"All people climb the same mountain. The mountain, however, has many pathways – each with a different view. A person knows and understands only what he sees from his own pathway, and as he moves, his view will change. Only when he reaches the top of the moun-*

tain will he see and understand all the views of mankind..." *Hawaiian History, Tales from the Night Rainbow,* By Pali Jae Lee and Koko Willis

(11)   *"By believing passionately in something that still does not exist, we create it. The nonexistence is whatever we have not sufficiently desired."* Nikos Kazantzakis

(12)   *"For as he thinketh in his heart, so is he."* Proverbs 23:7 King James

(13)   *"Every moment of your life is infinitely creative and the universe is endlessly bountiful. Just put forth a clear enough request, and everything your heart desires must come to you."* Shakti Gawain

(14)   *"Let a person radically alter his thoughts, and he will be astonished at the rapid transformation it will effect in the material condition of his life."* *As a Man Thinketh,* James Allen

(15)   *"You are today where your thoughts have brought you; you will be tomorrow where your thoughts take you."* *As a Man Thinketh,* James Allen

Addl. The Virginia Satir quote on self esteem, *MY DECLARARTION OF SELF-ESTEEM,* (chapter 12) is used by special permission of her ongoing Virginia Satir Global Network. www.satirglobal.org The quote is from Virginia's book *Self Esteem.*

Acknowledgments

The first person I must thank is Robin who spent nearly as many hours as I on this project. Robin helps manage much of my life leaving me the time necessary for creativity and public speaking. Thank you Robin! And C.K. is Robin's daughter. Thank you C.K.!

The main person who gets credit for the manifestation of this book for you all is my dear wonderful, beautiful Оля (Olya). Оля and I met in December of 2006. It was some kind of love at first sight. We knew something had happened, then it set in after a few hours and continues to do so. After some time, not long, two or so children were decided on as the desired number. I had to become un-retired and get back to some serious work for this new largest endeavor of my life.

The Objective is Happiness was started in NIkolaev, Ukraine a couple days after a birthday party for Оля,

Autumn 2007. Thank you.

I must also thank my wide variety of friends with whom I have had the pleasure of walking short and long distances. I am so glad the game of life is infinite! We have so much to see and experience. *TW*

About the Author

"Live in Awe!"

— Thomas Wakefield

Tom is one of life's cheerleaders. You will hear him say often, life is astounding and incredibly awesome. "I do not understand how anyone can possibly become bored, there is so much with which to play!"

Tom has range, rock and roll to opera, backyard barbecue and sushi, under water and sky high.

Tom's first job was delivering pizzas. Except, we must go back a few years to the first time Tom hitchhiked west to Grandfather Fred's farm near Hatfield, Minnesota the day after school let out for the summer.

This was the routine for several summers, which contrasted life in the suburb of manicured lawns, Edina. Tom will tell you these were happy times. Driving field tractors, animals everywhere, taking things apart and putting them back together, things like whole engines.

It was a lot of "stay up as late as you can and early to rise" for one dollar a day, six days a week, with room and board for pay. Grandma's cooking was the best, and particularly her peanut butter cookies. Tom learned to drive everything with wheels by the age of 12. At summer's end, back to the institutional reality of school and the city.

Tom grew up thinking he would be a lawyer. Mom talked him into show business with television first followed by radio and the rest. He still studies law to this day.

Tom spent some years in construction and most of his life has been with words. "As a disk jockey one must become adept at saying the same things in new ways, hour after hour, five or six days a week."

Mixed in with radio in the '70's, Tom decided to disprove astrology and knew he had to learn it to accomplish that. A funny thing happened on the way to the argument and the short story is he ended up teaching astrology, which developed into classes on other spiritual phenomena.

Tom spent time in theatre as an actor, some time in television in nearly every possible capacity, and a couple years on the West Coast near Hollywood doing Hollywood things on a small scale. His company, Hollywood Resume, was a success. "I would have stayed, but the air suggested another view."

From radio, Tom entered the human potential movement. This was just after a lady named Virginia Satir, became a family friend. Fun how things just come together. Human potential at that time was seminar after seminar after seminar, and the radio career ended.

Tom moved to Hawaii for some college where he studied the Hawaiian language and Huna teachings from a real live kahuna, Joe Pahukula.

Tom's first publication was *Personal Excellence*, a three-tape cassette program.

Tom's first of three firewalk experiences was in the late seventies with Tony Robbins followed by another, which lead him to putting on a firewalk seminar where Mom, a sister, and an uncle, among others; all participated. He will tell you, doing that firewalk seminar was multiple defining moments.

The early '80's was the time of "Neuro Linguistic Programming training" (NLP), followed by mid '80's training in "Other than Conscious Communication" (OTCC), Dave Dobson.

One spring day in 1989 instead of driving past an airport, Tom drove in. In this moment of spontaneity, Tom made the decision to get his pilot's license and 51 flying hours later, he had it. The 51 hours is true, and the whole truth is, there were several hundred hours at the airport sitting in the left seat of every different airplane studying the controls. Tom has single and multi-engine certificates and ratings in land and sea planes.

Another day sailboat instruction began and Tom is now mono-hull and multi-hull trained, and is a sailboat and marine navigation instructor.

Tom lives on five acres in Minnesota where he raises peafowl (peacocks and peahens) and has chickens, cats and a dog.

Tom's *Welcome to Saturday Morn*ing© training seminars are training relative to any aspect of life. The reason Tom claims any is that the very basics of human communication and energy are taught, and addressed as they apply to life energy and getting results.

Websites in development:

The book
The Objective is Happiness,
        The Art and Law of Attraction

http://theobjectiveishappiness.com

The seminars, coaching, and training
Welcome to Saturday Morning

http://welcometosaturdaymorning.com

Printed in the United States
150547LV00001BA/3/P

9 780982 239759